MICROWAVE THE BOAT ASHORE
Comic Relief from Everyday Life

Illustrations by **Mary Chambers**

Microwave the Boat Ashore

Comic Relief from Everyday Life

Ken Alley

Harold Shaw Publishers
Wheaton, Illinois

ISBN 0-87788-553-2

Edited by Elizabeth Cody Newenhuyse

Cover design by David LaPlaca

Library of Congress Cataloging-in-Publication Data

Microwave the boat ashore : comic relief from everyday life / [compiled] by Ken Alley.
    p.   cm.
  ISBN 0-87788-553-2 (pbk.)
   1. Christianity—Humor. 2. Church—Humor. 3. Church—Anecdotes. I. Alley, Ken.
  PN6231.C35M53   1999
  230'.002'07—dc21

                                                    98-55386
                                                    CIP

04   03   02   01   00   99

10   9   8   7   6   5   4   3   2   1

Contents

Acknowledgments 7

Introduction 9

1 "Mom, a Grader Hit Me!" 11
   Real Life with Kids

2 The Cow That Went Home to Mama 21
   True Tales of Love & Marriage

3 Created from an Apple 29
   Wisdom from Church Kids

4 "Who Gives This Mother Away?" 41
   or, Out of the Mouths of Preachers

5   More Awkward Christian Soldiers..................................47
    Stories from the Back Pew

6   Cooking the Worshipers 55
    More Stuff People Have Typed Wrong

7   "Dr. Seuss Will See You Now"..................................61
    or, It Happened in the Doctor's Office

8   On the Road..69
    (and Off the Wall)

9   Why Do We Park on the Driveway and Drive on the Parkway?.......77
    Random Observations and General Silliness

Acknowledgments

A special thanks to Sara Dinkelman
whose oddball sense of humor parallels my own.

Introduction

While collecting stories from around the country for my earlier humor book, *Awkward Christian Soldiers,* I received hilarious anecdotes about daily life. These were too good not to share!

Each day we face the world and all the obstacles life throws at us. What if we had a new perspective? What if we began to see the fun in our lives, if we allowed the things that stress us to make us laugh?

Your daughter's permanent marker drawings on the basement floor become priceless works of art. The doctor who kept you waiting for two hours last week has a plumbing emergency—and you're his plumber! Life can be sweet. Look closely, lighten up, and enjoy!

"Mom, a Grader Hit Me!"
Real Life with Kids

The walking embarrassment

My thirteen-year-old daughter and I were standing at the curb of our town's Main Street waiting for the big Fourth of July parade to begin. I was leaning on a tree, feeling pretty good about life in this great land of ours, and then my daughter nudged me. "Look!" she whispered, pointing across the street to a face in the crowd. "There's Jessica Jones. She's one of the popular girls. Look better!" Jessica Jones, naturally, had no idea we were even there. But then I remembered being thirteen years old and the agony of being seen in public with my mom. I stood up straight, smoothed my hair and "looked better." At least that's what my daughter said.

E. N.

Designated no-hitter

The baseball coach gave strict orders for the short-for-his-age, eleven-year-old batter not to swing at the pitches. Because of his small strike zone, he almost always walked. Since there were two outs and the next batter was a power hitter who would more than likely drive in some runs, the coach didn't want to risk the little guy's striking out. Right before the kid went up to the plate, the coach reminded him one more time, "Just stand there and don't swing!" The boy asked in all seriousness, "Do I even need to take the bat with me?"

S. D.

Take that

My husband knocked and entered the bathroom where my nine-year-old daughter was brushing her teeth after taking her shower. He asked if she was ready for bed and she said she was. He said, "Whoops, looks like you forgot to pick up your towel." As he exited and closed the door, he saw her give the towel a kick and say, "Bad towel."

A. D.

And they're off!

When we were driving in the Omaha area, I pointed to the greyhound track and announced to my eight-year-old daughter, "Look, Shelby, that's where they have dog races." She looked, then in a voice dripping with sarcasm said, "Right, Dad, like anybody's gonna ride a dog."

M. E.

Now, that would hurt

My kindergartner came home from school with a black eye. When I asked what happened, he replied, "A grader hit me." Picturing one of those huge road grading construction machines, I gasped, "A WHAT hit you?" "You know," he replied, "a first grader."

G. R.

Thinking out loud

While I was teaching high school, the students came in and seemed to be unusually noisy one day before class. Finally I looked at them and said, "Sssshh! I can't hear myself think!" A lad in the front row quipped, "Think louder, Miss T!"

I. T.

In the doghouse

My four-year-old son, Bobbie, was playing in the kitchen with our new puppy, Mollie. He asked my wife, "How does Mollie laugh?" My wife answered, "She wags her tail."

A little later, after being naughty and getting sent to his room for punishment, Bobbie sat pouting. Mollie came bounding in, happy to see him, wagging her tail. Through his angry tears, Bobbie yelled, "What are you laughing at?"

M. A.

Taking the bait

One hot summer day, my buddies and I decided to go fishing. It hadn't rained in a long time, so we knew it was going to be hard digging down to find any worms. My cousin Kirk suggested, "Let's just do some fly fishin'." In complete sincerity, my fifteen-year-old sister asked, "How are you gonna catch any flies?"

K. S.

Anybody home?

My husband and I were in the process of getting divorced. The ordeal was especially hard on our young son, Cole. One night when he was really missing his daddy, I suggested that Cole give him a call. The phone rang and rang and I gently suggested that we try back later because Daddy probably wasn't home right now. Cole wasn't ready to give up, so I let him listen to it ring about twenty times more before I said, "He's just not there now; we'll have to try later." Cole sighed, but suddenly his face brightened and he said, "Wait, Mom, I think I hear footsteps!"

S. O.

Good question

I was waiting in line at the check-out when my eight-year-old son excitedly whispered, "Mom, Mom," and motioned me down to his level. "Mmmmf mmmf

MMMF!" he mumbled into my ear. "What?" I asked. Again, "Mmmmf mmmf MMMF!" I shook my head. "Slow down and try again," I said. He rolled his eyes and sighed, then, "Mom . . . that . . . girl . . . is . . . DEAF!" he whispered slowly.

"Oh," I said, noticing the people in the next aisle were using sign language. "Then why were you whispering?" I asked my son.

B. D.

One-way dialogue

I was driving down the highway taking my seventeen-year-old son to church camp. It was a six-hour trip one way, but I always felt it was worth it. I was feeling mellow and thankful for my son; he's a good kid whom I haven't lost much sleep over. Always home on time, always called to let us know where he was, friendly and compassionate, president of his junior class. . . . I could see him with my peripheral vision, and I assumed he was just daydreaming. So I decided it was a good time to tell him how proud I was of him, how happy I was that he was my son, and so on.

After five minutes of my sharing my deepest feelings, I noticed that he hadn't said anything. I assumed I had touched such a sensitive chord in him that he wasn't sure how to respond. Looking at my son more closely, I realized that his eyes were closed, his headphones were on, and he was listening to the music from *Star Wars*. He hadn't heard a word I said.

A. K.

Real cool

The last week of my freshman year in high school I finally got up enough nerve to say "Hi" to this gorgeous hunk senior quarterback . . . and my gum fell out of my mouth.

L. M.

Who is that guy?

I had a beard from the time my son was born until he was four. One day I shaved it off, and of course it was a real shock for him to see me beardless. I overheard him asking my wife, "Mom, did you know Dad had a face under there?"

M. H.

Parental instructions

As we dropped our son off at college, his last words to his dad were, "Please wear things that match."

L. B.

NO, DAD. CLOTHES *FROM* GAP – NOT CLOTHES *THAT* GAP.

Turnabout

My thirteen-year-old son and I had an argument the other day. He stormed out of the room and yelled, "I wish you were never born!"

L. S.

Gene pool

My little girl asked, "Mom, do I come from your side of the family or Dad's?"

S. J.

Looking sharp

When I was young my mom once hollered at me, "Don't look at me in that tone of voice!"

Just kidding

It was fun putting a regular egg in the hard-boiled bowl until my kids caught on and started doing it too.

If your kids won't eat yogurt, put it in a bowl and tell them it's pudding.

The Cow That Went Home to Mama

True Tales of Love & Marriage

He just doesn't get it

After listening to a female Ph.D. lecture our class on gender sensitivity, my husband leaned back and said sincerely, "She's pretty smart for a woman."

S. O.

An ounce of prevention

My wife is so sweet when she wakes up in the morning. Her first words to me are usually, "Don't start."

Hiss . . . hiss . . .

Have you and your spouse ever had a "whisper fight"? You know, those times when you just have to argue about something, and your kids or your guests are in the next room.

Henpecked

My mom was taking what was left of a watermelon out to the chickens. When she got out to the coop, she decided one of the leftover pieces was too good to throw to chickens. She stood right there among the birds and finished the good piece while the chickens ate the rest. So there she was, in the chicken pen, eating with the animals! My husband, Jim, has never let her live this down. He even bought her a craft novelty picture of chickens eating watermelon.

J. M.

But women ask directions

I got my wife's car all packed for her eight-hour trip to her sister's in Minneapolis. She had been looking forward to this for a long time. I kissed her goodbye, hoping that she would have good weather and not get lost, but I figured that with only two major interstates to follow, she'd be fine. As she was backing out of the garage, she waved good-bye, then stopped, rolled down the window and asked, "What's the highway that goes left at Des Moines?"

K. A.

Phew, that's a relief

My wife was having some sinus trouble and, while sleeping, she would exhale like a quiet air hose. Early one morning, I woke up and heard a continuous hiss. I couldn't believe she could exhale for such a long time. I felt sorry for her, then became concerned as the hiss continued far too long. *Breathe!* I thought. I finally realized that the city workers were outside blowing out the cracks in the street with an air compressor so they could be filled with tar. I thought it was her. Duh.

T. R.

Hair apparent

My friend recently got married. I didn't know her husband that well, and I always thought of him as "that bald guy" because he shaved his head. They moved away and when I saw her a year later, she was with another man. Short-lived marriage, I thought, until I realized it was the same man, but now he had hair.

The cure for marital spats

My wife and I were having an animated discussion about getting a new hot water heater. She finally screamed, "I NEED a bigger watt hotter heater!" That kinda took the steam out of her argument.

B. H.

Counting their chickens

I'm a real estate agent in a small town in the Midwest. One day I was showing a house to a couple in their seventies. I could tell they really liked the house and I would probably get the sale, but privately I wondered whether they could really afford the place. Well, maybe they were selling a farm, I guessed. At the end of the tour, I asked, "Well, shall we say this house is sold, pending loan approval? Or were you going to pay cash?" The wife smiled shyly and turned to her husband. "Should we tell him?" she asked. The husband said sure. The woman then turned back to me and said, "Well, the truth is, we just got a letter from Publishers Clearing House Sweep-

stakes, and—we're in the final drawing!"
K. K.

Diet deception

My cousin was on a strict diet, but she lost control one afternoon and binged on half a chocolate pie when no one was around. She immediately felt guilty and knew her husband would give her heck for falling off the diet wagon. When her son entered the kitchen she managed to "accidentally" flip the pie plate off the table, and it landed upside-down on the floor. "Oh, no!" she exclaimed. "I dropped the WHOLE PIE!" She baked a new pie for the family, the kids backed up her story about the first one being

destroyed, and her husband never knew the truth.
B. A.

Milking an argument

The young bride had been given a family cow as a wedding gift. During the first few months of marriage, the couple had the usual newlywed disagreements, and the wife would often load up the cow in the pickup and drive home to Mama. This happened so frequently that the story started going around that whenever the cow heard a ruckus in the house, she would jump up into the truck bed.
B. M.

Advice that works

If your wife says, "You don't have to do that," do it anyway. If your wife says, "It doesn't matter," it matters.

Ouch

I gave my wife a good-bye hug this morning and said, "Thanks for working so hard." She responded, "Somebody's got to do it."

P. O.

Created from an Apple
Wisdom from Church Kids

Good question

After my four-year-old daughter concluded her prayer with "Amen," she looked at me and asked, "Why can't I say, 'A-woman'?"

S. O.

Thanks for sharing that

Right after I became a Christian and turned my life around, I was roped into teaching my daughter's preschool Bible class. I wasn't sure how she would react having her dad in charge—and, to be truthful, I wasn't quite sure what I was getting into. The class was discussing what they did to help their moms and dads. My daughter kept waving her hand and I finally (and reluctantly) had to call on her. She said, "I help my daddy when he's watching a ballgame." As much as I didn't want to, I had to ask her to explain. She said, "I help you not to say ____ and ____!" She ripped them off just like I used to.

L. N.

Livin' water, y'all

The question for the confirmand was, "Jesus spoke with a _____ at a well about living water." The correct response was "Samaritan woman." The unexpected answer from one confirmand was "Southern accent."

K. M.

Stop the wedding!

My six-year-old son said he was going to be the ring "barrier" at my wedding next month.

S. O.

The perils of outreach

As I was sitting through a rather lengthy sermon, my daughter's little neighborhood friend who was sitting with us yelled out, "I HATE CHURCH AND SO DOES MY DAAAAD!" I thought I was going to dissolve.

J. M.

Pulpit nightmare

I remember when the preacher's kids took their dad's sermon notes out of his Bible one Sunday morning and replaced them with comic book pages. As I recall, the church floors were sure polished for a long time after that incident.

K. H.

Plea for deliverance

My three-year-old daughter was being very naughty during church, worse than usual, and to keep her still during the upcoming prayer, I decided to pin her between my knees. In the quiet before the prayer, she folded her hands and prayed out loud, "Dear Lord, you gotta help me, I'm trapped!"

J. A.

Shattering the silence

Right after a prayer my baby brother burped so loud I thought the windows were going to break.

L. C.

Creation interpretations

One preschooler said that Adam and Eve were created from an apple and unleavened bread is made with no ingredients.

My five-year-old daughter kept telling us about "Adam and Steve" in her Sunday school class. It took a while before we figured out she meant Adam and Eve.

D. M.

I was teaching my son's kindergarten Sunday school class and asked who the first man and woman were. One kid said, "Adam and Eve." My son responded, "No, it's Mary and John"—meaning Joseph. Not only did my own kid give the wrong answer, but his wrong answer was wrong.

S. B.

She must have been hungry

In his sermon, my pastor mentioned

something about winter coming on and how we had all better be getting our sheep gates in order. My six-year-old daughter said, "Sheet cake?" At least she was listening . . . sort of.

J. J.

Make sure it's grape juice

A lady who was a member of the church but had not attended for several years decided she would repent and go every Sunday again. She took her ten-year-old son along with her. The woman took communion as it was passed around, and passed it over her son's head. When the collection plate came around, she put in a quarter. After the first Sunday service, someone asked the boy how he liked church. He said, "It wasn't bad, but next time I'm going to bring a quarter and get me some of those refreshments."

Solemn sacrament?

While standing in line receiving communion during Mass, my husband was behind me holding our fifteen-month-old son. He was asleep, but he kept having outbursts of laughter as if he was dreaming of something funny. I turned around to see what was going on (I thought my husband was tickling him) but decided there was nothing we could do. He would start, then stop, then start again. People were starting to get amused, and we knew things were getting out of control when the priest started to laugh. We were so embarrassed.

B. F.

Sunrise service

My daughter's family used to attend a church where everything was quite informal. The pastor wore a suit rather than a robe, and the congregation dressed casually. Then the family moved to a different city and joined a church where things were more formal. The women of the congregation wore dresses, the men wore suits and ties, and the pastor wore a fancy robe with formal accessories. The first time my five-year-old grandson saw the pastor, he exclaimed, "Why is that man wearing his bathrobe?"

Shout to the Lord

We were in church and the congregation was singing a rousing favorite hymn, putting into it all the joy and vigor it deserved. In the silence following the grand ending, my five-year-old son took his hands off his ears and shouted, "Why is everyone singing so LOUD?"

D. M.

Next time, bring coloring books

We were in for an extra-long church service and everybody knew it. It was

"Rally Sunday" on the Lutheran church calendar. This meant extra hymns, extra Scripture readings, special music, and so on. Our seventy-year-old assistant pastor had to handle these duties since our regular pastor was guest-preaching elsewhere. I've always wondered why a pastor can't find a way to keep the sermon SHORT on church holidays, but he seems to enjoy the captive audience, and instead really gives it his best. About fifteen minutes into the sermon, my seven-year-old daughter looked up at the elderly minister and loudly whispered to me, "Doesn't his voice get tired of talking so much?"

G. J.

That's telling 'em

One Sunday in church when my daughter was three-and-a-half, we sat in front of two elderly ladies who carried on a conversation throughout the service. Finally my daughter was fed up. She turned around, stood on the bench, and whispered, "Will you please be quiet! This is God's house and I can't hear."

J. C.

So where did Cain's wife come from?

I'm a preacher's kid, but I've decided to take the advice of a friend of mine, also a PK. She suggested we refer to ourselves as TOs (Theologian's Offspring).

Of course, with this title comes much responsibility. My best friend would often comment in Sunday school class, "Your dad is the pastor; you should know the answers to all the questions."

B. R.

What a guy!

When my three boys were small I got into the habit of putting them down for their naps shortly before 2:00 every day so I could watch my favorite soap opera in peace. As my older boy reached the age where he didn't need naps anymore, he was allowed to stay up and play quietly. I never thought he paid any attention to my show, which would surely be considered boring to a five-year-old boy. But when I picked him up from Sunday school one week, his laughing teacher related that she had asked the children if anyone knew who Philip was. My son confidently told her, "Philip's the guy with all the girlfriends on 'Guiding Light.'"

Kids' praise

During the singing of "Let All the People Praise Thee," I remember my three-year-old brother screaming out ever so sincerely, "LET ALL THE PEOPLE CRAAAAZY!" He was a lot of fun in church.

C. L.

It's all God's, anyway

My daughter wondered whether, since President Kennedy was Catholic, it would be okay to put a Kennedy half-dollar in our Methodist collection plate.

C. L.

Out with the bath water

My wife was giving our newborn his bath, and my daughter was watching. Suddenly she came running to me and hollered, "Dad, BJ's biblical cord fell off!"

D. M.

Overheard: One kid singing, "Microwave the boat ashore, alleluia . . ."

How not to reach kids

As the lesson leader wrapped up a long children's sermon, he dismissed the youngsters by saying, "Come back again to learn more about Jesus." At least half the congregation saw one young boy shake his head and reply, "No way."

Really ecumenical

As we were passing through a small town, my daughter said, "That's weird. That sign says it's a Baptist Catholic church. I've never heard of such a thing." We turned the car around for another look. The sign said, "St. John the Baptist Catholic Church."

J. F.

Priorities

One little girl always started her prayers with, "God bless me, God bless Mommy and Daddy . . ." and so on. She remarked to her mom, "Do you know why I say God bless me first? Because I like me best."

J. B.

Splash!

My dad was the pastor in our Baptist church, so I was used to playing in the sanctuary. The place just never held much reverence for me, since I spent so much time at the church, waiting for Dad, doing small cleaning chores, hanging around. My buddies loved it when I'd in-vite them over to the church to play. We'd have a foot race down the aisles and end it with a cannonball into the baptistery.

D. U.

Dad's job

The focus of the church school lesson was on family, particularly the idea that Jesus grew up in a family and his earthly father was a carpenter. I asked, "Does anyone know what a carpenter does?" All was quiet until six-year-old Alexis proudly responded, "One who lays carpet?"

C. D.

Those PKs!

My husband, a preacher's son, would stick straight pins up through chair cushions in the church foyer and hide in a nearby closet to watch the people sit down.

S. S.

Pssst! Pass it on!

I was in church with my young daughter and the congregation was "passing the peace." We shook hands with worshipers who were sitting nearby and murmured the greeting, "Peace be with you." I had often noticed that when the entire congregation is involved, this activity creates a low, rumbling hissing sound. My daughter tugged at my sleeve and whispered, "Daddy, why does everybody say, 'psss, psss, psss' when they're shaking hands?"

R. S.

Well, it's better than Thessalonians

When Phillip was three, his Sunday school teacher had her first baby and named him Luke. That afternoon when Phillip's daddy came home, his mother told him to tell his daddy the new baby's name. Phillip scrunched up his face, trying to remember. "Matthew?" he asked. "No," came the reply. "Mark?" "No." Then he beamed and shouted, "Romans!"

F. M.

"Who Gives This Mother Away?"
or, Out of the Mouths of Preachers

Low cost of living

While counseling a transient member on job opportunities, the pastor asked if he had any money. He said he was flat broke. "You don't even have a hundred dollars tucked away somewhere?" the pastor queried. The man replied, "If I had a hundred bucks I wouldn't need a job."

J. A.

Wrong bride

At a wedding rehearsal, the pastor came to the point in the service when the father is asked, "Who gives this woman away?" He was looking at the bride's mother at the time and inadvertently asked, "Who gives this mother away?" It woke everyone up, including the pastor.

M. P.

The overall picture

Early in my ministry I was asked to make a presentation on banner making. I was trying to get the women to be more concerned with the overall effect than with the fine details. I looked right at them and said, "Forget all the little details and pay more attention to the big overalls." Most of them were farm wives and knew quite a lot about overalls of all sizes.

Quick recovery

One time my father was preaching hot and heavy about Samson. Dad told about Samson's adulterous affair, about having his eyes plucked out, and the rest. To continue his story, he intended to use the phrase "beast of burden." However, somehow he got his syllables mixed up and said, "They made him a burst of burden! A beast of beaden!" By this time the congregation was in an uproar. Dad sighed and said, "Oh well, he was a strong man."

R. W.

A toast to the happy couple

At the Kevin Hamm and Michele Egging wedding, the preacher said, "We are not only joining two fine young people in matrimony, but we are also joining two fine families, the Hamm and Egg . . . ing families."

J. H.

Creature comforts

The elderly dean of a Christian college was addressing the student body about living the life of a Christian. He spoke about the life of John in the New Testament. He said, "We need more Johns around here!" Everybody became uncorked, but the old fellow didn't have a clue why.

S. R.

Close to the truth

In his sermon, the pastor admonished the congregation that the prohibition against telling falsehoods was "the most important commandment." After a moment's thought, he qualified the statement: "Well, maybe it's not the most important, but it's right up there with the top ten."

D. F.

Legalism

I was at a wedding where the pastor said, "in the name of the law" instead of "in the name of the Lord."

Water hazard

One preacher was unable to climb out of the baptistery because he flooded his waders while bending over to lift a new convert up from the water.

T. N.

At least not in church

One pastor was talking of the importance of various talents of church members. Without every gift, he said, "The eyes can't hear, the ears can't walk, the feet can't smell . . ." That was as far as he got because the congregation erupted into laughter.

Real reverence

While discussing Moses and the burning bush, our pastor read, "And God said, 'Moses, you're on holy ground, take off your feet.'"

Career change

At an installation service in Oregon, it was announced that the new minister had "served time in Texas."

Heard at a wedding: "Will you take this man to be your wife?"

More Awkward Christian Soldiers

Stories from the Back Pew

A really friendly church

As I stood up for the benediction, all four buttons on the back of my dress popped open. A nice male friend of mine gently buttoned them and all was well until after the service when I turned around to thank him and found out it wasn't my friend, but a visitor.

D. H.

Media ministry

We have a song director who also has a radio show on the local station. One Sunday he said, "The prayer after this song will be brought to you by Jerry Simon of Simon Auto Sales."

B. J.

Star power?

On the marquee in front of the theater, the movie was advertised U FORGIVEN, with Clint Eastwood. The *N* had fallen down.

K. A.

Man of few words

During one wedding ceremony I attended, the groom was so emotional that he couldn't recite his vows. The pastor had to change things so he could just nod his head, yes or no.

L. R.

Second fiddle

Our youngest daughter is a natural teacher and loves being with young children. One year during high school she helped with Sunday school and for the entire year, we would enter the church to a chorus of young whispered voices saying, "There's Angie!" "Mom, Dad, it's Angie!" "Look, there's my Sunday school teacher, Angie!" It was a bit humbling to be known as the Sunday school teacher's dad after I had spent nearly twenty-five years teaching there myself.

Testing, testing

Because the wedding was being video-taped, the pastor held the microphone in front of the couple so their vows would be clearly recorded. The nervous groom leaned forward and said, "Hello?"

L. R.

A dealer you can trust

When I walked through the church parking lot I noticed a van that had a JESUS decal stuck next to the DODGE emblem. It looked like an advertisement for "Jesus Dodge." I had never heard of this dealership, but I bet you would be treated fairly there!

K. A.

Putting God first

The bride suggested to the organist that she play some favorite hymns prior to the processional. Right before the bride was to walk down the aisle, the organist played, "I'd Rather Have Jesus."

Furry friends

I'm the principal of a small Christian elementary school. One morning before school, I visited the cook in the kitchen and was horrified when she told me she'd seen a big rat. "It even sat up and looked at me before it ran away and hid!" she exclaimed. She related that she'd called her husband and he had already managed to kill and remove the rat.

Unfortunately, my relief was short-lived. Thirty minutes later at our morning chapel service, I got a sick feeling in my stomach when our fifth-grade teacher made the announcement that their class hamster had escaped during the night. Sometimes I hate this job!

R. B.

Better than Sea World

I'm a member of a very large congregation. Our baptistery is, by necessity, huge, and is fully encased in glass. One Sunday there were several converts to be baptized. The pastor and the male converts entered from the men's changing room on the right, and the female converts entered from their changing room on the left. After the pastor baptized the first male convert, the man started wading off to exit on the left. Our pastor called to him and said he must exit through the same door that he had entered. To the delight of the congregation, the convert ducked completely underwater and swam to the appropriate door.

J. B.

Closed for repairs?

Over the massive front doors of a church, these words were inscribed: "The gates of Heaven." Below that was a small cardboard sign that read, "Please use other entrance."

Blind faith

I was flipping through the TV channels rather quickly and stopped at one that had a minister praying. His eyes were closed, his forehead furrowed, and he looked to be in deep conversation with God. My wife asked me what channel that was, and I told her, "That's the blind channel." She remarked that she didn't know there was a special channel for the blind, but thought it was a good idea. (I was just kidding, dear.)

S. N.

Lack of vision?

The song leader had just gotten new glasses. He walked up to the podium without his glasses and announced that the next song would be "Standing on the Promises," on page 502. He got the page number correct, but it was not the song he mentioned. When the congregation began to chuckle, he put on his glasses and discovered his error. On page 502 was the song "Open Mine Eyes, That I Might See." He grinned and said, "Maybe if I would open mine eyes I would get it right."

D. W.

Our song leader announced that we would be singing "the first verse of hymn 143." Opening his hymnal, he added, "That's because it's also the ONLY verse of hymn 143."

Listen up

One man said his favorite part of the worship service is when the preacher says, "And in conclusion. . . ."

Cooking the Worshipers
More Stuff People Have Typed Wrong

Heartless congregation

As a secretary for my church back in the early 1980s, I was asked to type a flyer that announced an upcoming event. I agreed, but we later realized that my typing skills were a little off because the flyer read, "We do things with out love" (instead of "with our love"). The worst part was that several people had proofread the flyer, but no one caught the mistake until several hundred had been printed.

D. W.

Bulletin bloopers

After Sunday services we will be serving Kentucky Fried Children.

Needed: Love seat for counseling center.

Please bring an offering and a snake to share.

The Food Pantry needs food. Michelle, who runs the pantry, has fun out of money to buy food.

As we bring this child through baptism into the Kongdom of God . . .

Area panty donations were approved.

We invite everyone to the insulation service for the new pastor.

Don't forget the potluck after services. Bring your foot and put it on the center table.

For Sale: Used church lights. Contact pastor during the day.

Church kitchen bulletin board: Egg Dippers—Make sure you cover your bottoms. (Of your Easter eggs, that is.)

The preacher training workshop promotes the featured speaker as "recognized for expertise ineffective instruction."

With sixty faulty members, it's the largest seminary in the world.

One church apparently found a way to measure the impact of its sermons. It recently announced, "Blood pressure screening before and after the service."

The new church will be located where Lutherans are most dense.

The topic for the Elders' Bible Class will be "Sinplicity of Christianity."

"To meet again in that home where there will be no sorrow, no death, and no rears."

Youth group activities will be gin at 3 P.M.

The meeting was called to order and the financial secretary gave a grief report.

At 7 P.M. tonight come to the sin-a-long with Pastor.

A brief business meeting and conversion with the speaker is planned.

May the Lord look upon you with flavor and give you peace.

Bring something for yourself and someone else to barbecue.

Those interested in sinning in the Reformation service chorus, join us for rehearsal.

Singles on the church roof were examined. We have some on hand and will replace them next spring.

L.W. will pray for weeds in the parking lot.

Our sanctuary is now air-conditioned for the summer months and is cooking our summer worshipers.

Our best wishes to Gene and Joan who were untied in Christian marriage.

A special memorial service will be held for members who have died during the past two years at both services.

Envelopes need to be stuffed with senior volunteers for a congregational mailing.

"Dr. Seuss Will See You Now"
or, It Happened in the Doctor's Office

Oh, by the way . . .

I examined a seventyish gentleman whose history was basically devoid of any illness or accidents. When I looked at his x-rays, however, they were horrible! "Your bones look like you were run over by a truck!" I exclaimed. "Oh yeah," he said. "I was. I forgot."

S. A.

Easy for them to say

The person who said, "Laughter's the best medicine," didn't ever have abdominal stitches.

The last straw

At the end of a very tiring day at the office, an elderly lady struggled through the front door with her cane. I thought to myself, *Please, not now, I'm ready to go home.* She said her mother was out in the car and was having a hard time walking, and she wondered if I would take a look at her.

T. C.

Rx: Green eggs and ham

A four-year-old girl came into my office with her grandma. I told her that I knew her mommy so be sure to tell her that Dr. Alley said hi. As they were leaving I reminded the girl and asked if she remembered my name. I prompted, "Dr. What?" She thought for a moment and said, "Seuss?"

K. A.

It's a miracle

I told a patient that I wanted to see him again on Friday. He replied, "I can't make it Friday because I have a funeral to attend. My cousin died again last week." I asked, "He died again? When did he die the first time?" He laughed and said, "What I mean is, another cousin of mine died last week."

K. A.

In layman's terms

- An elderly gentleman came in complaining of "hardening of the artilleries."

- Another patient complained of having "very close veins."

- Yet another described his medication as "that peanut butter ball" (phenobarbital).

He'll try to fit you in

When I first started my practice, things were pretty slow for a while. After a few months, business was picking up nicely, and

I felt I could afford to hire a receptionist and let my wife be a homemaker again.

Still, there were numerous open appointments on the book. The first time the new receptionist answered the phone, someone asked her what openings were available for that day. "Let's see," she began. "Nine-fifteen, 9:45, 10:15, 10:45, 11:15 . . . " and on and on, all the way to 5 P.M. and the day's last appointment. After she hung up, I let out a loud, "NOOOOOO!"

D. D.

Don't forget their heartworm pills
Two of my five children were due for childhood inoculations. My husband wanted to come along, so of course it turned into a family outing. After the children were finished, my husband was paying the bill and asked if the doctor's office would send reminder cards when it was time for another child to have a shot. The receptionist smiled patiently and said, "No, it's really up to the parents to keep track of that."

My husband insisted, "But I'm positive we've gotten reminder cards in the past." At this point I stepped up and quietly told my husband that those reminder cards had been from our veterinarian regarding our dog.

K. B.

Mr. X

On the sidewalk in front of my office, I found a sheet of six identical photos of a man. I didn't recognize him, but thought maybe one of my clients would, so I taped up the photos by the reception desk. After a week, no one had said anything, until late one afternoon an elderly lady stopped in and looked at the photos. My receptionist asked her if she knew the man pictured. The lady didn't answer right away, but kept examining the photos. Soon she said, "I'm not sure, but I think I know the man in the upper right-hand corner."

I still don't know if she was pulling my leg or not.

T. A.

Rescue 911

I was treating a patient one afternoon when I heard an ambulance with sirens blaring pull up in front of my office. I went out to see what was going on and saw flashing lights on the rescue unit, along with a police escort. *This is great for a practice*, I thought. I asked what was up and the paramedic hollered through the window, "Is Burch in your office, Doc?" (Burch was another paramedic.) I said he was and I was giving him a treatment. The paramedic asked me if I would get him real quick; they had an emergency heart attack call and had to have him, pronto!

S. B.

When it doesn't pay to get out of bed

I spent the better part of an afternoon looking for a phone number I desperately needed. I had written it down on something and forgotten about it until I needed it, and then, of course, I couldn't find it.

I finally located the number and yes, it was right in front of me. In order not to lose it again, I asked my bookkeeper to toss me the highlighter marker. I pulled off the cap and made a couple of deliberate swaths across the phone number—and realized the bookkeeper had given me the black magic marker by mistake.

Some days . . .

T. C.

Incoming!

As I was walking through a parking lot on a hot summer day, I noticed an elderly lady sitting in her car. She was rubbing her head, but otherwise seemed okay. I did some quick shopping, and when I came back I saw this lady still in the same position. I decided to see if she needed assistance and knocked on the window. She didn't react, so I opened her door and asked, "Are you okay?" She answered, "I've been shot and my brains are coming out."

I was shocked, but didn't see any blood, so I told her to remove her hand and let me examine her wound. She was hesitant, but finally let me look. I discovered the funniest thing: a biscuit tube had exploded in her grocery sack (because of the heat, I suppose). One of the biscuits had become a projectile and smacked her in the back of the head and gotten tangled in her hair. She actually thought a gun had gone off and she had been wounded.

L. U.

Professional opinion

After I finished the treatment on a middle-aged lady, she jokingly said, "Doc, you really messed up my hair." I jokingly said back to her, "No way, it was a mess before you came in here." I haven't seen her since. (Oops!)

T. S.

Good suggestion

I am a chiropractor, and one of my patients suggested I call my office "Twist & Shout Chiropractic."

K. A.

Over the hill?

An eighty-year-old patient told me, "I'm not sore because I'm eighty years old. I'm sore because I water-skied all day yesterday."

One elderly gentleman said, "The next big break I get will probably be my hip."

Hmm... I'D SAY TAKE TWO ASPIRIN AND GET A PERM

On the Road
(and Off the Wall)

Wish you were here

While vacationing in London I was going to send a postcard to some friends back home in the U.S. Not knowing how much postage to apply, I asked the hotel clerk, "What should I put on this?" He said, "Oh, just put that you are having a good time."

E. P.

Judge not . . .

During a recent out-of-town business trip, I was killing time in a restaurant before an appointment with a client. I figured I had plenty of time before my meeting, but I was appalled at the poor service, lack of attention, and overall attitude of my waitress. I looked at the wall clock and said to the guy sitting next to me, "Look, their clock is an hour fast. I can't believe how inept these people are." The guy smiled and said, "The clock's right. Daylight Savings Time went into effect at 2 A.M." Well, I was a half-hour late for my meeting, lost a big sale, and decided I probably shouldn't be critical of others anymore.

G. L.

Let the traveler beware

I was stationed for two weeks' duty at an Air Force base in Japan. I arrived on a commercial flight late one night and took a cab to the base. It seemed to take forever, and all the driver would say was, "Many mile . . . many mile." After forty-five minutes, we finally arrived and I paid the cabby his $65 fare. It was a bit steep, but I didn't have a choice. After my two weeks were up, I hailed a cab to take me back to the airport. I'll be darned if it wasn't the same driver. I settled back for the long drive, but in ten minutes we pulled into the airport. He said, "Ten dollars." I asked him why the trip had taken so long and cost so much when he took me to the base two weeks ago. He replied, "Win some, lose some." I'll bet he never uses that phrase again.

D. F.

To tell the truth . . .

I was sitting in a big airport terminal watching a couple of rambunctious pre-schoolers run, jump, fight, and climb themselves silly. Their grandparents were sitting close by, and although they looked exhausted, you could see the love and affection in their eyes. I struck up a conversation with them by saying, "It looks like you've been baby-sitting awhile." The grandmother smiled sweetly and said, "I can't wait to get the little brats home!"

C. W.

Sucker!

I got tickled while visiting my sister, Bettye, on her farm in Kansas. They have a mongrel dog who was hit by a truck a few years back, and because of this accident, the dog hobbles around on only three legs. My sister and I were walking back from the garden and Missy the dog flopped down on her back right in front of her. Bettye stopped, reached down, scratched Missy on the stomach, and said, "Missy, you goof. Ever since your accident, you think all you have to do is lie down on your back and I'll stop whatever I'm doing and scratch you on the belly." I said, "Bettye, Missy's probably thinking, *Bettye, you goof. Ever since my accident, all I have to do is lie down on my* *back and you'll stop whatever you're doing and scratch me on the belly.*"

K. A.

Definition of camping: Going to a lot of trouble to make yourself miserable.

Never say never

My wife and I misread our airline tickets, missed our flight, and ended up waiting twelve hours on standby for another one. We swore we'd never be so dumb again . . . because we have done this before.

R. Y.

Buried treasure

My wife and I were on vacation at South Padre Island, Texas, where the beaches are beautiful beyond words. I looked at all that sand and had a vision of finding an old Spanish doubloon washed up on the shore. One day while my wife was sunbathing I took a long walk on the beach, drinking in the scenery and indulging my "Spanish coin" fantasy. Suddenly I stopped and gasped. There it was! My coin! I gently picked it up out of the sand. I washed it off and found out that I am now the proud owner of a 1992 Lincoln penny.

S. G.

Navigational aids

I've always been impressed by airline pilots. I'm amazed by how they can control a huge aircraft from that cramped cockpit and know what all those dials and gauges mean. I figure their powers of concentration and sense of direction must be fantastic. I was thinking about this recently as I watched the flight crew leave the jetway and enter the airport terminal. As the pilot exited the jetway, he paused in the gate area and waited for the flight attendant to catch up with him. She then tugged on his sleeve and gestured to her right. "Oh. This way?" said the pilot. So that's how they do it!

A. K.

Drives you up a wall

The ultimate personal race—getting your seat belt buckled before the dinger stops on its own.

My wife drives around with the top down on her convertible with the air conditioner on.

It's a good thing they post those "Bump" signs along the highway; you can almost feel some of the bumps.

Have you ever changed lanes at the same time a skidding noise came over the radio? Makes your heart stop.

Bumper sticker: Go ahead. Honk your brains out. It shouldn't take long.

These English signs were spotted in various foreign countries:

- *Tokyo hotel:* It is forbidden to steal hotel towels. If you are not a person to do such a thing, please do not read this notice.

- *Paris hotel elevator:* Please leave your values at the front desk. If you lose them in your room, we are not responsible.

- *Athens hotel:* Visitors are expected to complain at the office between the hours of 9 and 11 A.M. daily.

- *Moscow hotel:* You are invited to visit the cemetery where famous Russian and Soviet composers, artists and writers are buried daily except Thursday.

- *Japanese hotel:* Cold and Heat. If you want to condition the warm in your room, please control yourself.

- *German campsite:* It is strictly forbidden on our Black Forest camping site that people of different sex, for instance, men and women, live together in one tent unless they are married with each other for that purpose.

Why Do We Park on the Driveway and Drive on the Parkway?
Random Observations and General Silliness

One of those days

Why is it that when you need your umbrella to get from the house to the car, it's in the car; and when you need it to get from the car to the house, it's in the house?

Have you ever been in the shower and dropped a new bar of soap on your foot?

My roommate looked into the mirror early one morning and said, "I look like I've been sent for and couldn't come."

Don't you hate it when you raise your garage door from the inside and last night's rain drips down on you?

Have you ever poured a big bowl of cereal, added sugar and your favorite fruit, and then discovered that you're out of milk?

When you can't locate that wasp, do you ever feel like it's sneaking up behind you?

I locked my keys in my car and ended up walking three miles home for an extra set . . . which reminded me of the spare key that was in my wallet.

Don't you hate it when you check your computer monitor and discover you've been typing capitals for the last five minutes?

Growing up?

I always wished someone would make Big Wheels for adults.

When I was at the end of my rope with my kids not letting me take a nap, I decided to write my mom and tell her how sorry I was for never letting her take a nap.

At what age should you stop blowing the paper off straws?

Made of money

After years of shrewd investing, calculated saving, and counting my pennies, I've finally become independently poor.

You can usually generate some extra spending money when a family member hollers from the bathroom, "Somebody bring me some toilet paper!"

We're all broke, just at different levels.

A Cadillac Eldorado with a diesel engine pulled up next to me at a stoplight. If I was going to spend that much money on a car, it would *not* sound like a tractor!

Life's questions

Isn't it fun listening to people talk to their pets?

Really, what's the big difference between 1 percent and 2 percent milk?

How do penguins tell each other apart?

Why is there always one computer key that you don't know how to use?

Really, why *do* we drive on parkways and park on driveways?

How did they figure out how many dog years equal a human year?

Why do we have apple and peach *orchards,* but oranges come from *groves?*

What did they mean when they said the airplane was "forced to land on an unpaved portion of the runway"?

How can a restaurant advertise anything as being "homemade"?

"Place stamp here. Post office will not deliver mail without postage." What, some people don't know that yet?

What's the difference between partly cloudy and partly sunny? I guess it depends on whether you're working inside all day or going on a picnic.

JOE! YOU'RE A GENIUS!

You are what you eat

You know how the government has forced manufacturers to put nutritional information on all packaged food? Some junk food companies could simplify this job by printing "None" under the words "Nutritional Value."

My weight is perfect; it's my height that varies.

If you eat liver on purpose, think of what can happen by chance.

I read the ingredients on my can of Mandarin Orange Slice soda pop: "Carbonated water, high fructose corn syrup and/or sugar." You mean they don't know for sure what's in there?

On really windy days, I'm kinda glad I'm a bit overweight.

To get some quick energy, I ate a big piece of my mom's chocolate cake right before I ran the 120 high hurdles. I had to borrow a stepladder to finish the race.

There's a force within you that lets you know that you overate late last night.

Someone tried to make spinach taste better by making it into fettuccine. It didn't work.

I wish someone would invent a fruit that tasted like a greasy hamburger.

A local restaurant included on its Sunday menu: "Baked Fillet of Soul."

Hey! You want some cheese and crackers with that whine?

Say that again?

Quote from an FAA official: "We are retrieving everything on the ocean floor that's pickable upable."

Newspaper ad: February is National Wild Bird Feeding Month! (Okay, who thinks up this stuff? And do I need to buy a greeting card for this occasion?)

One businessman said, "I'm locking up early today because I'm coming in late tomorrow."

"The average age of Olympic hockey players is twenty-three or younger." (Well, which is it?)

A TV anchorwoman said, "The suicide bomber strikes again." (He must not be very good.)

During a very in-depth conference on computer function, the speaker ended his lecture by saying, "Now, is that thoroughly confusing?" One exasperated listener said, "Is WHAT thoroughly confusing?"

People-watching

Isn't it something how you think people who drive the wrong way on a one-way street are so stupid, until you find yourself doing it?

There should be a law that if anyone over thirty gets a bad sunburn he should have to pay a fine for being so stupid.

I saw a guy whose sweatpants were being held up by suspenders. . . . Now that's different.

Why do people walk on the street when they could walk safely on the sidewalk?

My two grown sons and I were sitting in a McDonald's restaurant when my younger son said, "Hey, Dad, that guy over there just put his whole tray in the trash receptacle."

How true

You know how good it makes you feel when you see your beautician's hair looking so cute? Well, somebody else cut it.

You have to get started if you want to get done!

Only in the English language could *fat chance* and *slim chance* mean the same thing.

Human nature is such a hassle.

One rule of life that covers about everything: If you're not sure, slow down.

When the going gets tough . . . the going gets tough.

People who snore always fall asleep first.

Happiness is waking up with the drudgery of going to work and remembering it's a holiday.

Having your yard plugged makes it look like a thousand dogs left their calling cards behind.

Swimming laps is about as much fun as poking yourself in the eye.

I bought a package of twelve pairs of crew socks, and on the package it instructs: "Remove from dryer promptly." Geesh, what's the worst that could happen, wrinkled gym socks?

Aging gracefully

You know you're getting older if you grunt every time you stand up.

This isn't a beer gut, it's reserve muscle.

If I was going bald, I wouldn't be so vain as to get a hair piece, have plugs put in, or ridiculously grow my hair long on the side and comb it over the top. I'd just maturely accept my fate and blow off the top of my head.

Good fences

I periodically add water to my neighbor's rain gauge and enjoy listening to him brag at the coffee shop.

L. T.

My neighbor wanted to borrow my new 2-cycle lawnmower to cut his yard so he could see if he liked how it ran. I told him, "Sure, but you can test it just as easily by mowing my yard."

S. T.

Keep your doors locked; it's zucchini season.

HEH! HEH! JUST STACK 'EM ON THE BACK PORCH HERE, GLADYS.

Time will tell

Instead of worrying about not getting my garden in on time, I plan ahead by not having one.

Sometimes I lose track of time . . . very conveniently.

I'm getting closer and closer to not being done.

I dragged myself out of bed this morning at 6:30 B.C. (Before Coffee).

Be a sport

Wouldn't it be funny if the third time a sportscaster replayed a fantastic catch a player made, the player dropped it?

I heard of a football team that was so bad their homecoming was scheduled as an away game.

Friends like these

Hey, you want to scare a person? Send someone a certified letter with a blank piece of paper inside.

Shall we dance?

There's a man who always punches in "The Laughing Polka" on the jukebox ten times, and then immediately leaves the lounge. If you've ever heard "The Laughing Polka," you'll understand why he leaves.

B. A.

Making headlines

I was sitting at the kitchen table in my underwear early one morning listening to the news when the anchorman said, "We'll have a look at you . . . I mean WITH you . . . at the national news in one minute." (Whew!)

T. P.

No interest

Even though I hadn't purchased anything with my VISA card, the company sent me a bill showing a balance of $0.00. The bill stated, "Minimum payment—$0.00. Payment due by May 17, 1997. Please remember that a late fee will be charged to your account if your minimum payment is not received by the due date, regardless of the amount due." I went ahead and sent them a check for $0.00. It was fun.

K. P.

Fore!

You know you've had a bad round of golf when you tell someone your score along with the phrase "or so."

Wouldn't it be awful if you got a hole-in-one and you were by yourself?

Seen on a T-shirt:
I hate golf.
I HATE GOLF!
Hey, nice shot.
I love golf.

I'll take your word for it
Yes, there is a book titled "Don't Squat with Your Spurs On."

Excerpts from the classifieds:

• Illiterate? Write today for help.

• Auto Repair Service. Try us once—you'll never go anywhere again.

• Dog for sale. Eats anything and is fond of children.

• Stock up and Save! Limit one per customer.

- Three-year-old teacher needed for preschool. Experience preferred.

- Toaster: A gift that every member of the family appreciates. Automatically burns toast.

- We will oil your sewing machine and adjust tension in your home for $1.

- Man, honest, will take anything.

- Used Cars: Why go elsewhere to be cheated? Come here first.

- And now, the Superstore—unequaled in size, unmatched in variety, unrivaled inconvenience.

- Bothered by dyslexia: Call toll free: 3511-256-008-1

Signs that make you wonder:

Sign on music director's door: Enjoy group singing? "Inchoir within."

Sign next to a small pond in a farmyard: "On Golden Puddle."

Oxymoron sign: Sanitary Land Fill.

Sign on restaurant: Wanted—Graveyard servers. (What, are they delivering?)

Two signs on a pole:
    Cemetery Road
    DEAD END

Sign in restaurant ladies' room: "These restrooms are cleaned 2x a day. If you have any questions or need help, please call 555-3368."

When you drive into a certain little town in central Nebraska, the "Welcome To" sign says: "Population 400 friendly people and 1 sorehead." (Several citizens took offense because each of them figured he was the sorehead.)
                    K. P.

Excerpts from actual letters received by a local welfare department in applications for financial support:

I am forwarding my marriage certificate and six children. I have seven but one died, which was baptized on a half sheet of paper.

I am writing the Welfare Department to say that my baby was born two years old. When do I get my money?

This is my eighth child. What are you going to do about it?

In answer to your letter, I have given birth to a boy weighing ten pounds. I hope this is satisfactory.

Unless I get my husband's money pretty soon, I will be forced to lead an immortal life.

You have changed my little boy to a girl. Will this make a difference?

In accordance with your instructions, I have given birth to twins in the enclosed envelope.

Just wait for it to get cold
Yesterday the wind-chill index was 20 below zero. Today it was 34 below. As a red-cheeked customer blew into my office today, he said, "Whew. It's sure not as hot out today as it was yesterday."

L. B.

I'll get the door
I hired a high-school boy to start working on my ranch. We were driving out to look at some cattle when I stopped, got out of the truck, and opened the gate to the pasture. I climbed back in the truck, drove through the open gate, stopped again, and told my new hired hand to "get the gate."

He got out, went back to the gate, and before I knew what he was doing, he lifted it off its hinges and loaded it in the back of my pickup.

It was going to be a long summer.

J. H.

About the Author

Ken Alley is the author of *Awkward Christian Soldiers*. He lives with his wife, Mary, in York, Nebraska, where he combines a chiropractic career with the pursuit of discovering the humor in all kinds of real-life circumstances. Ken and Mary have three children.

Ken is available for speaking engagements to churches and religious, civic, family and other organizations. To contact him for speaking or to send him stories, write P. O. Box 552, York, Nebraska 68467.

About the Illustrator

Mary Chambers's illustrations have appeared in numerous books, as well as magazines such as *Christianity Today* and *Leadership*. Much of her creative humor flows from being a pastor's wife and the mother of seven.